Rocket Phonics
First Steps

Activity Booklet

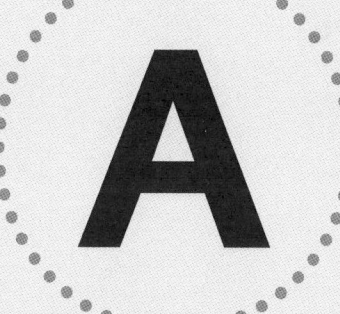

A

Abigail Steel

Name: _____

1. Say and colour the pictures.

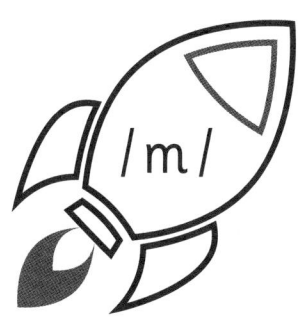  

2. Say the sounds and pictures.

m  m

3. Trace the letters.

4. Trace the word.

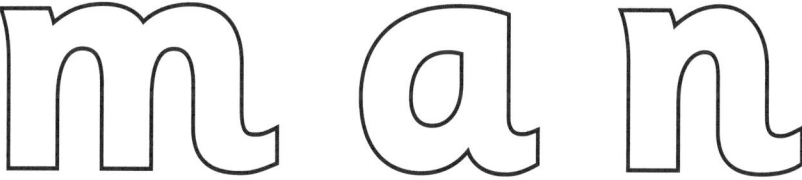

p

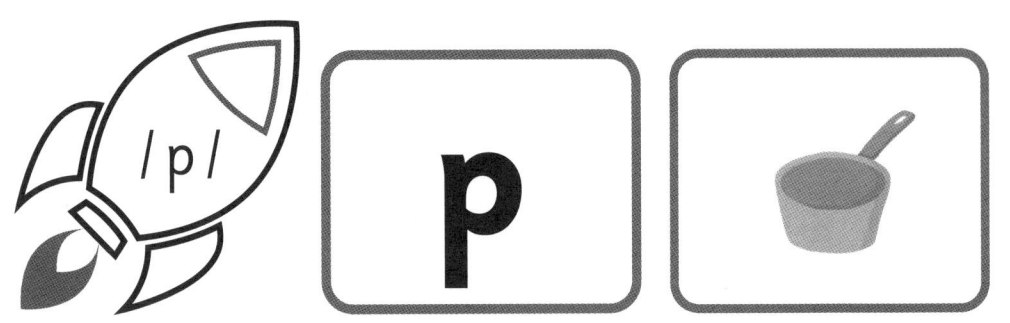

1. Say and colour the pictures.

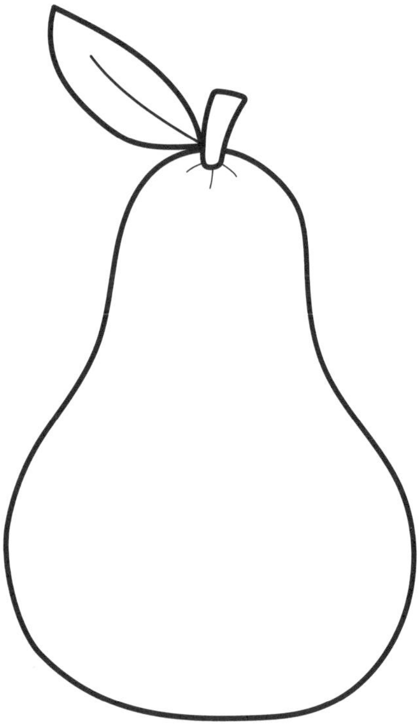

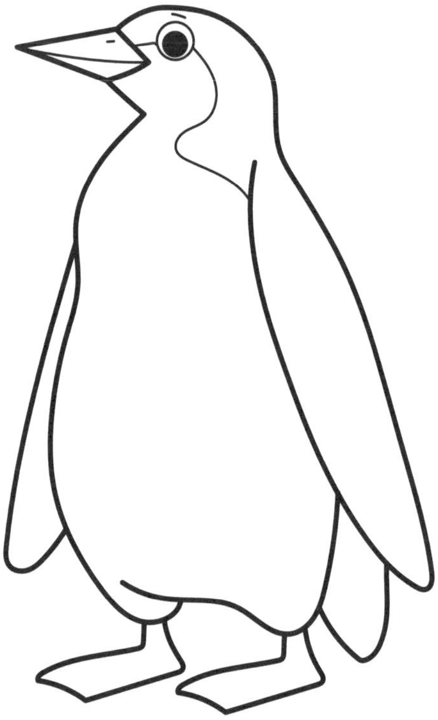

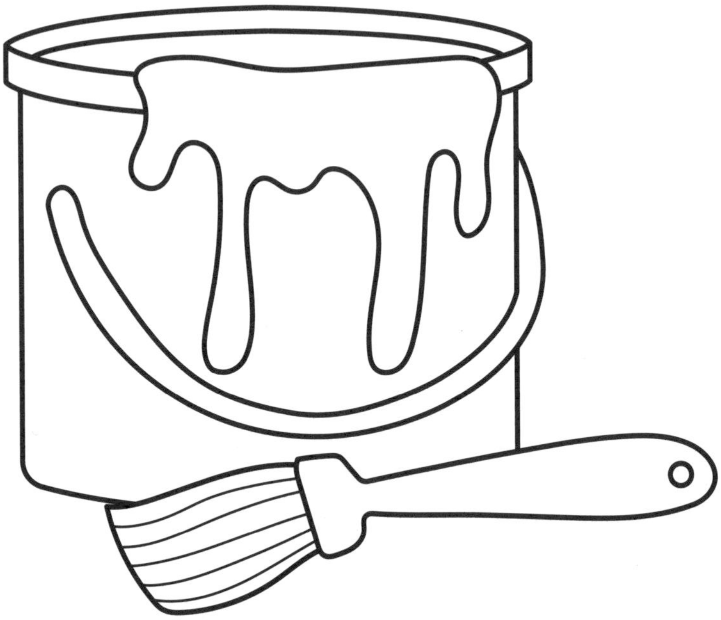

2. Say the sounds and picture.

 p   m   p

3. Trace the letters.

p   p   p

4. Trace the word.

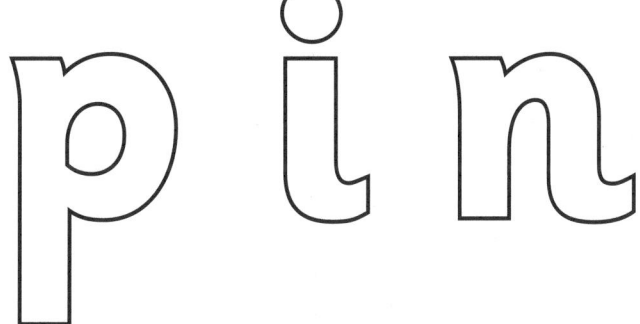

b

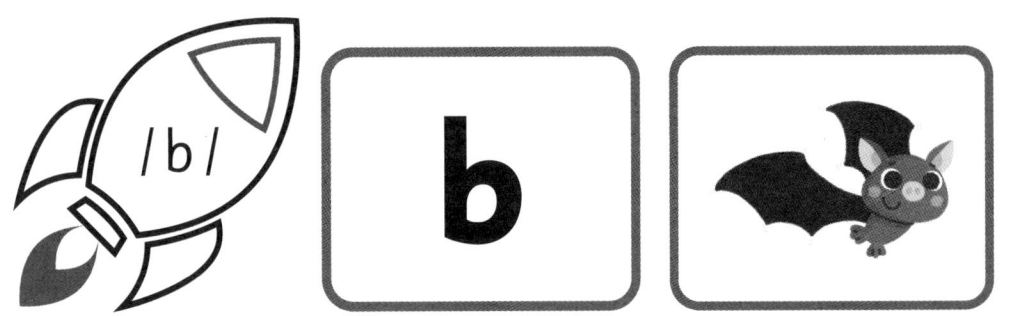

1. Say and colour the pictures.

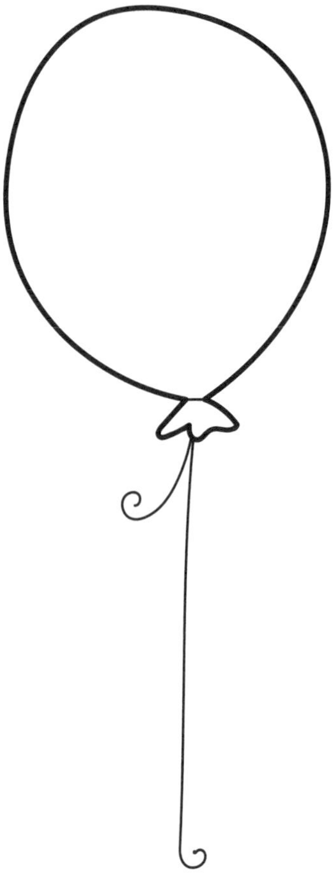

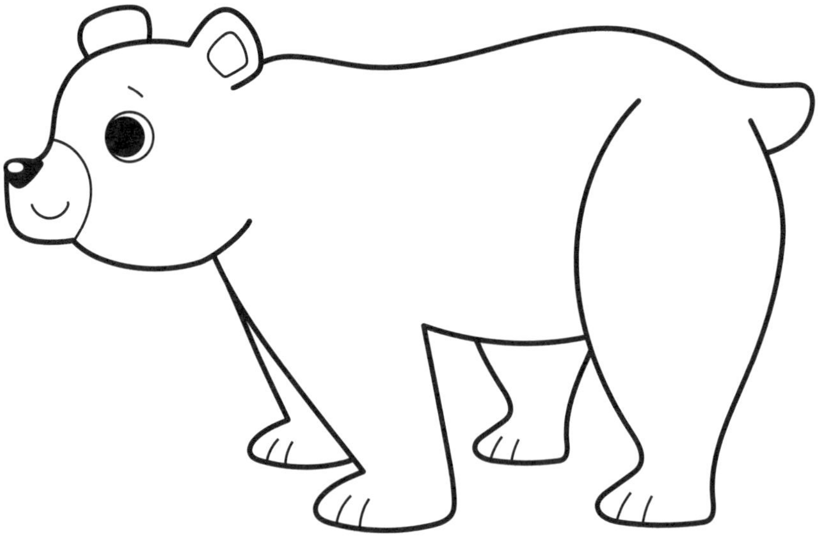

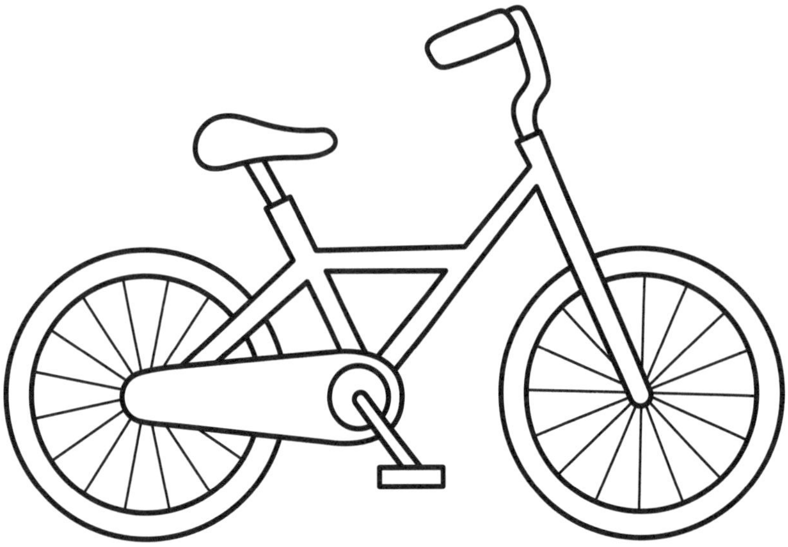

2. Say the sounds and picture.

b   m   p

3. Trace the letters.

b   b   b

4. Trace the word.

bag

n

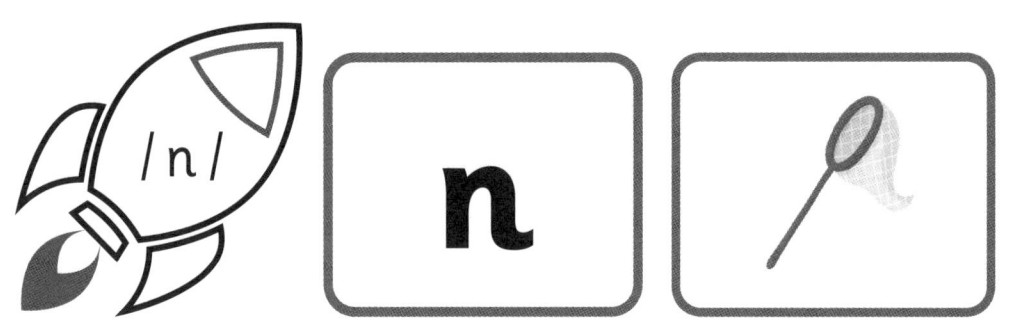

1. Say and colour the pictures.

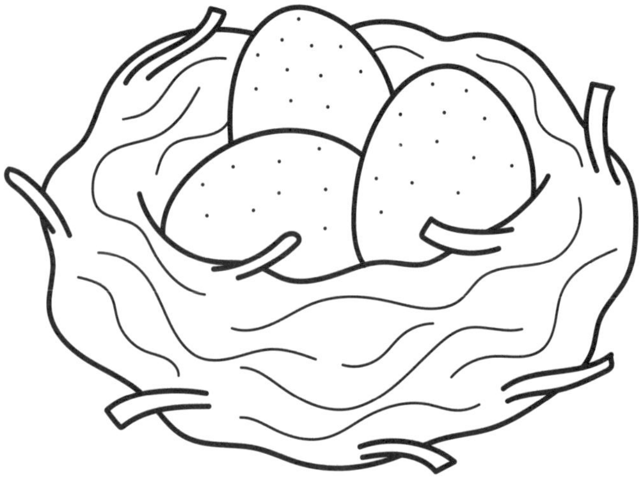

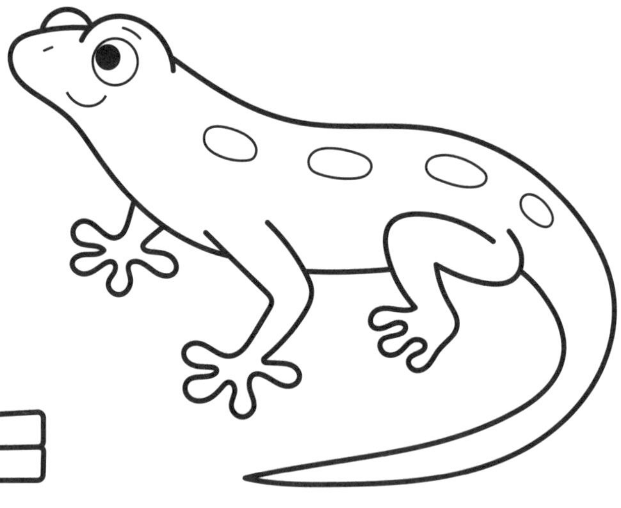

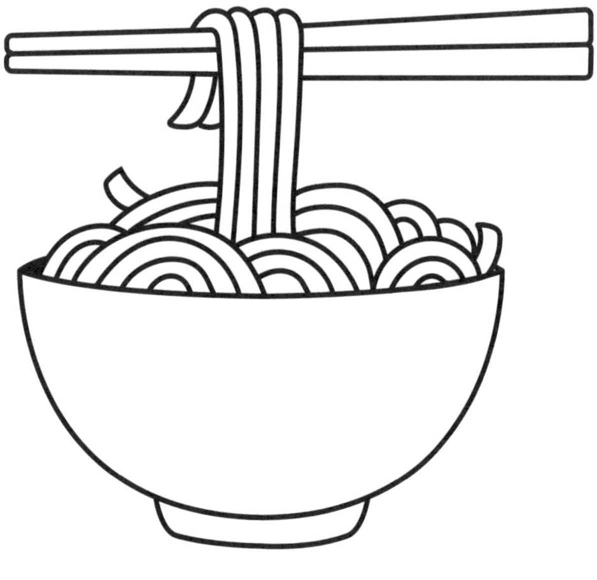

2. Say the sounds and picture.

 n b p

3. Trace the letters.

n n n

4. Trace the word.

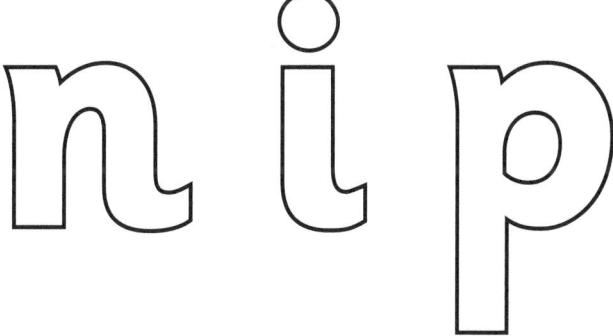

1. Say and colour the pictures.

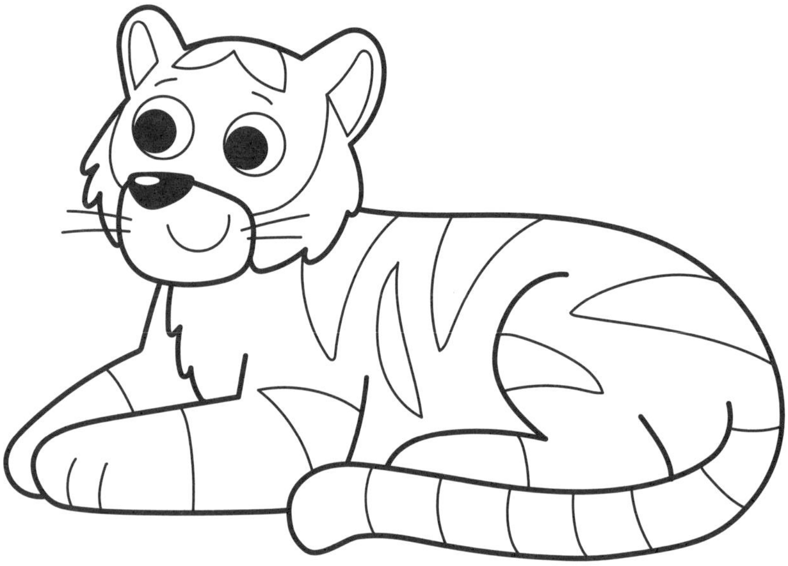

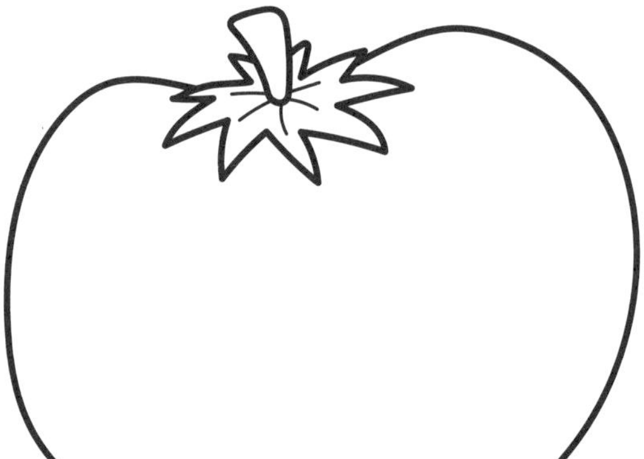

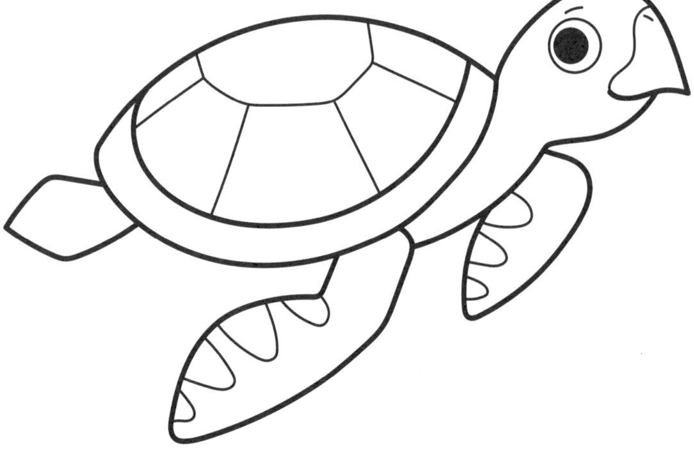

2. Say the sounds and picture.

t  n b

3. Trace the letters.

t t t

4. Trace the word.

d

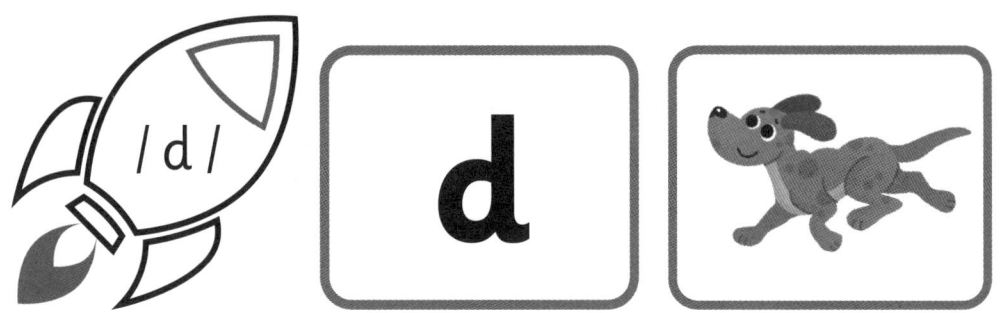

1. Say and colour the pictures.

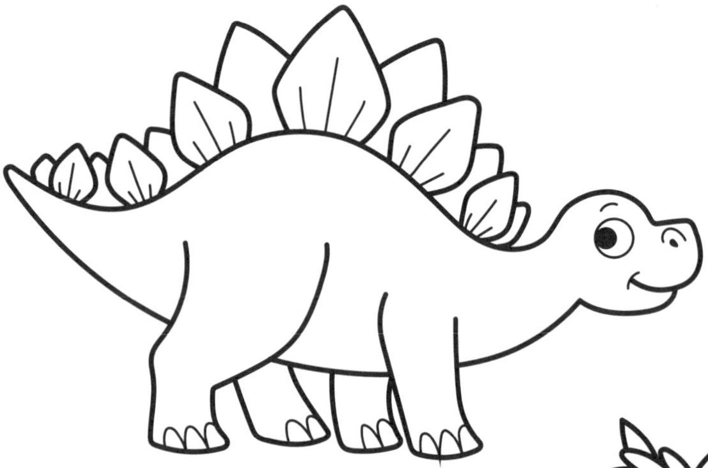

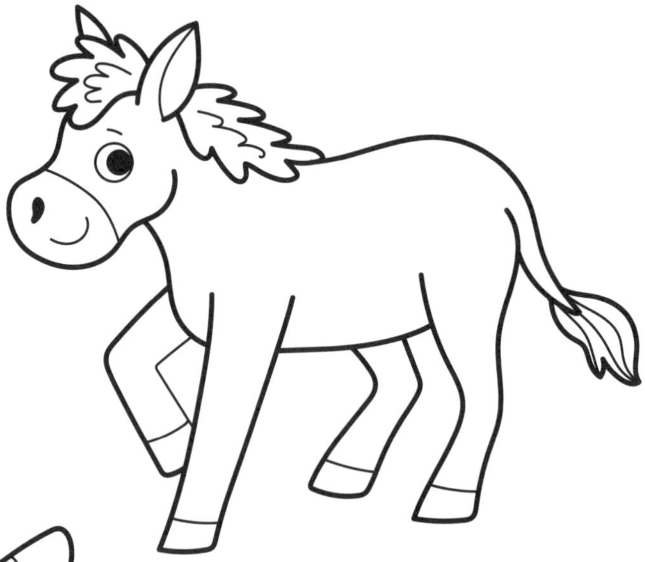

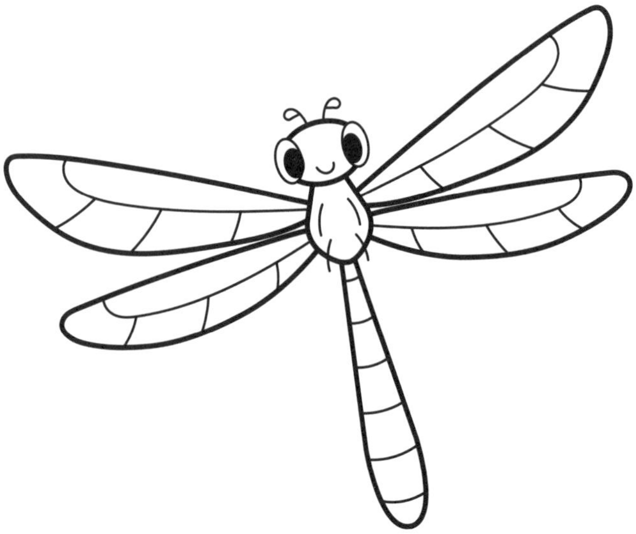

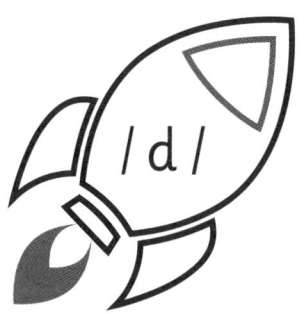  

2. Say the sounds and picture.

d   t   n

3. Trace the letters.

4. Trace the word.

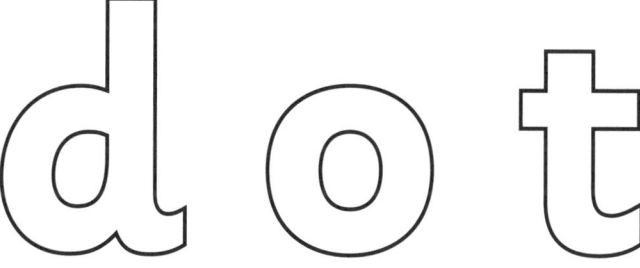

1. Say and colour the pictures.

2. Say the sounds and picture.

w   d      t

3. Trace the letters.

4. Trace the word.

h

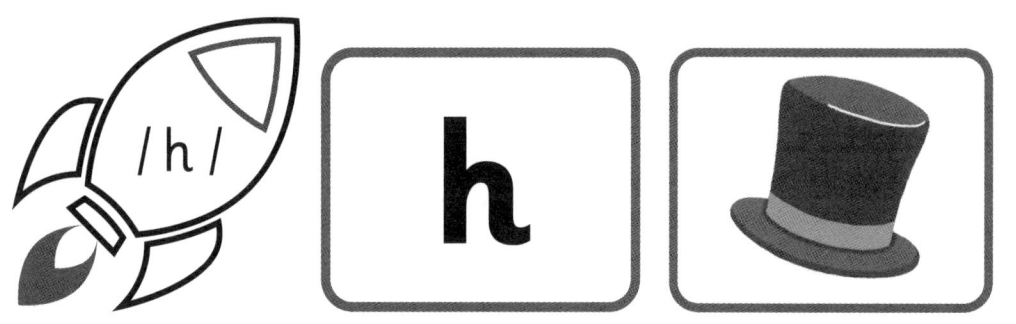

1. Say and colour the pictures.

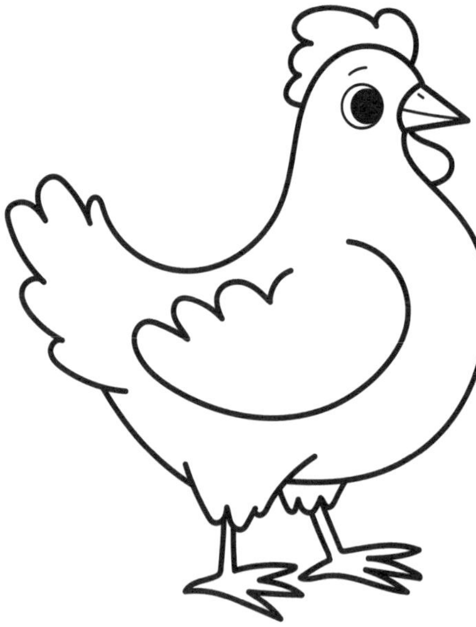

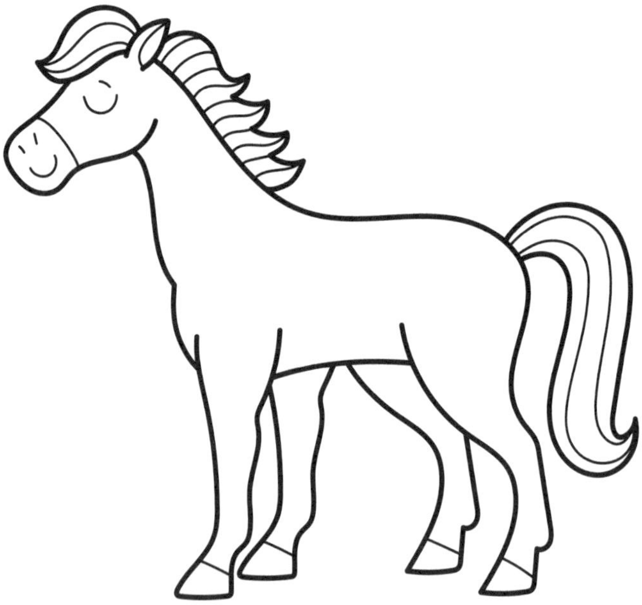

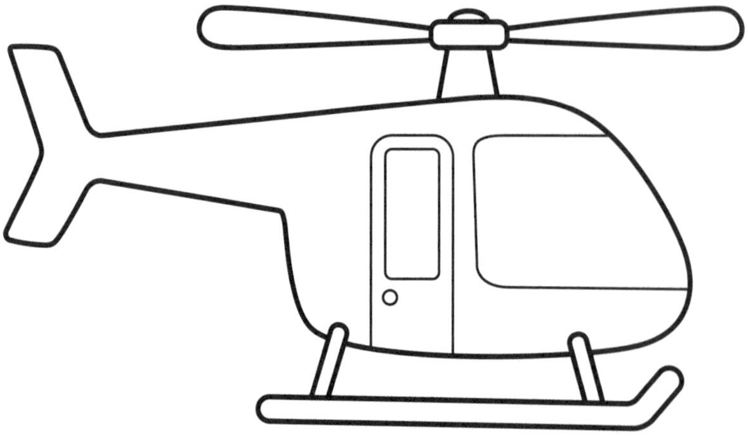

  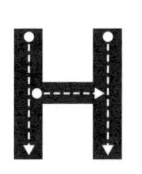

2. Say the sounds and picture.

 h   w   d

3. Trace the letters.

h   h   h

4. Trace the word.

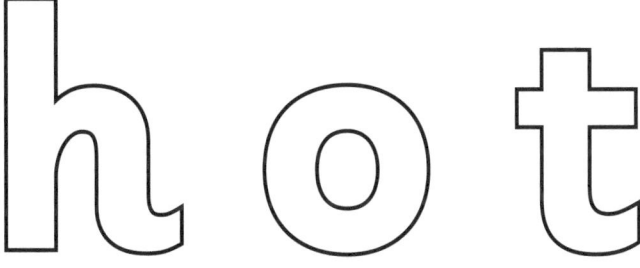

1. Say and colour the pictures.

 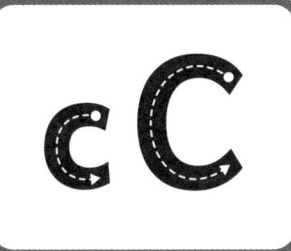 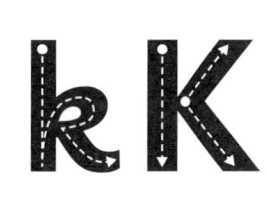

2. Say the sounds and pictures.

c    k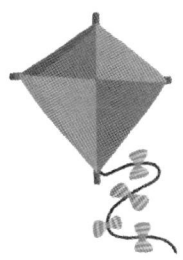

3. Trace the letters.

c   c   c

4. Trace the words.

cup kit

1. Say and colour the pictures.

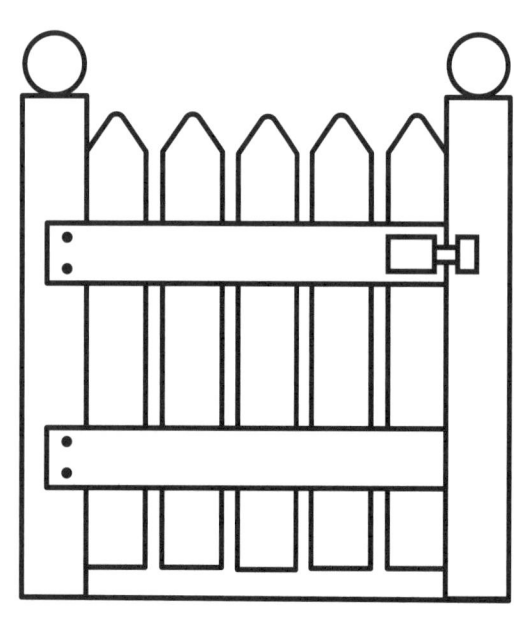

 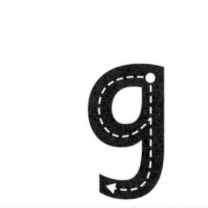 

2. Say the sounds and picture.

 g   c   k

3. Trace the letters.

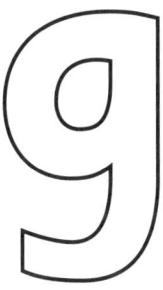

4. Trace the word.

 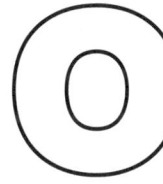 

1. Say and colour the pictures.

2. Say the sounds and picture.

f g c

3. Trace the letters.

   f   

4. Trace the word.

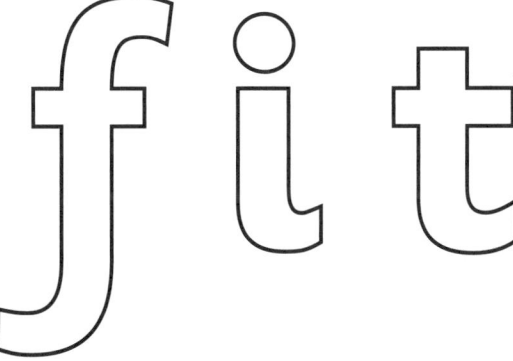

s

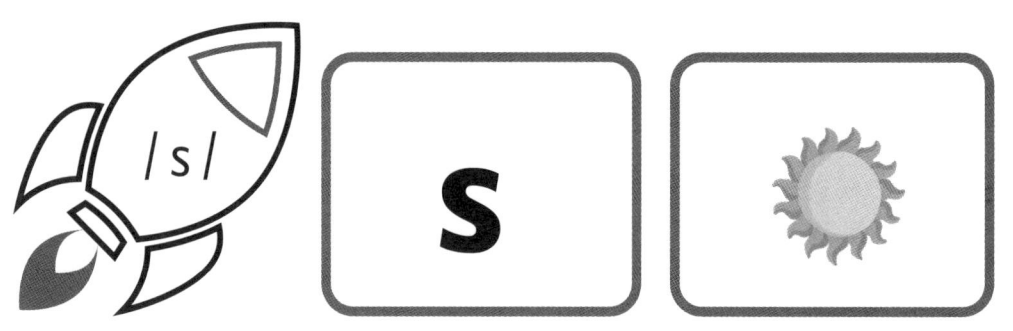

1. Say and colour the pictures.

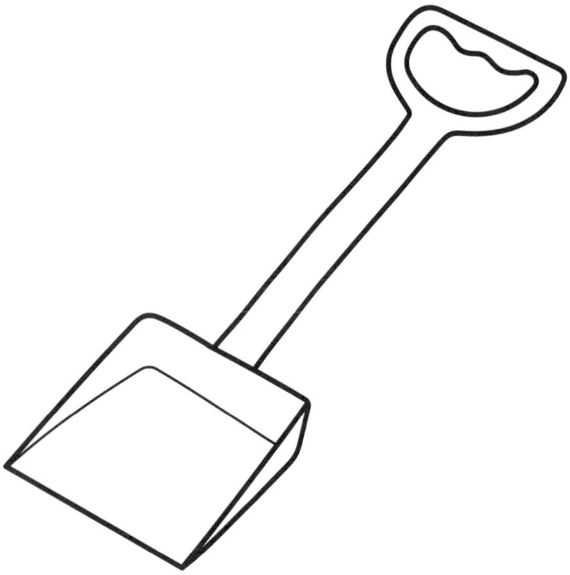

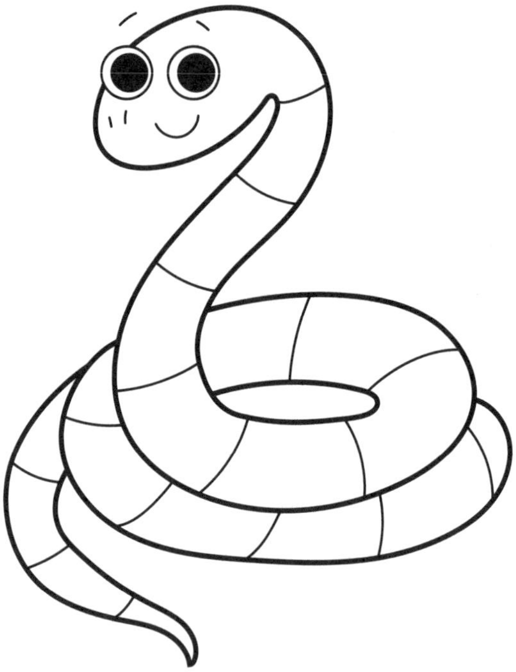

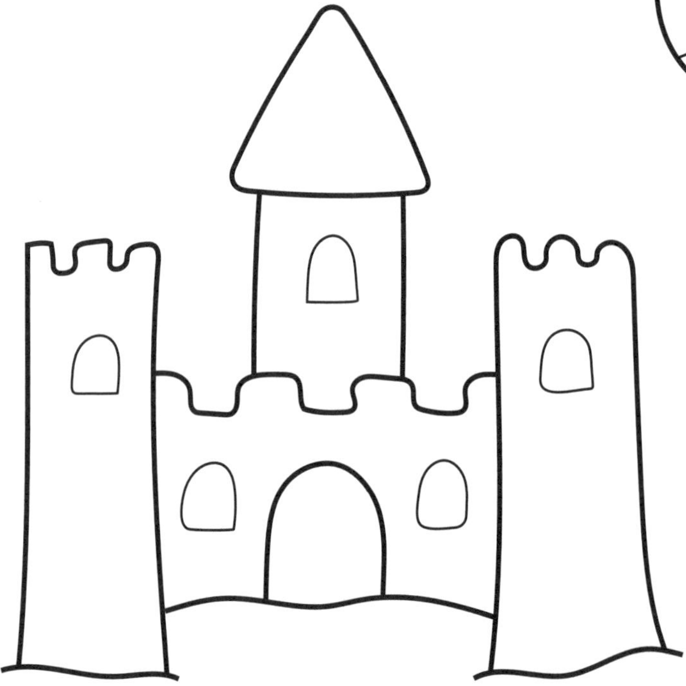

2. Say the sounds and picture.

s   f   g

3. Trace the letters.

 s   s   s

4. Trace the word.

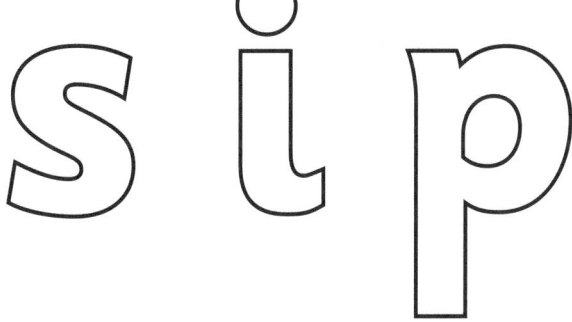

sip

1. Say and colour the picture and letter.

2. Say and colour the picture and letter.

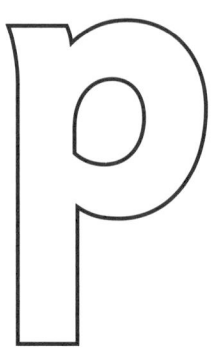

3. Say and colour the picture and letter.

4. Say and colour the picture and letter.

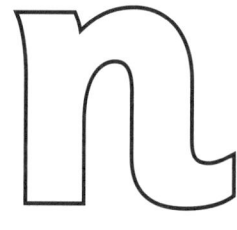

5. Say and colour the picture and letter.

6. Say and colour the picture and letter.

7. Say and colour the picture and letter.

8. Say and colour the picture and letter.

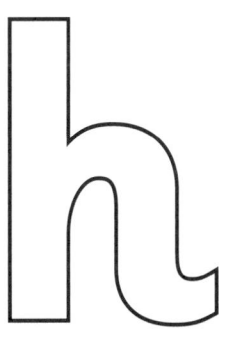

9. Say and colour the pictures and letters.

10. Say and colour the picture and letter.

11. Say and colour the picture and letter.

 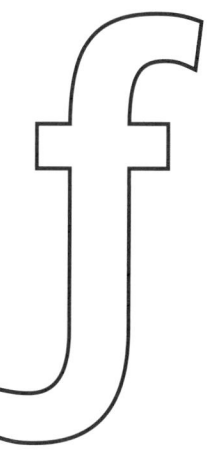

12. Say and colour the picture and letter.

Rocket Phonics: First Steps introduces young learners to the letters and sounds of the English language. The Activity Booklets provide enjoyable practice of early reading and writing skills, such as:

★ Recognising the initial sound in a spoken word
★ Linking the sound to its corresponding print letter
★ Blending the sounds in simple words
★ Building fine motor control through colouring pictures
★ Practising tracing letter shapes with a finger or pencil

The last section of each booklet provides a helpful review of the letter-sounds introduced.

Part of the Rocket Phonics First Steps teaching programme:
Online Subscription
ISBN 978 1 0360 0373 9

ISBN: 978 1 0360 0360 9
Text © Abigail Steel 2024
Illustrations, design and layout © Hodder & Stoughton Limited 2024
First published in 2024 by Hodder Education,
An Hachette UK Company
Carmelite House
50 Victoria Embankment
London EC4Y 0DZ
www.hoddereducation.com
Impression number   10 9 8 7 6 5 4 3 2 1
Year   2028 2027 2026 2025 2024

Author: Abigail Steel
Illustrator: Jake McDonald/The Bright Agency
Development Editor: Sasha Morton

With thanks to the schools that took part in development of *Rocket Phonics First Steps*, including: Boarshaw Community Primary School, Manchester; Boyne Hill CE Infant and Nursery School, Berkshire; Bradshaw Hall Primary School, Cheadle; Cheadle Heath Primary School, Stockport; Dairsie Primary School, Fife; Ebor Gardens Primary Academy, Leeds; Fibbersley Park Academy, Walsall; Shireland Technology Primary, Smethwick; Somerset Bridge Primary School, Bridgwater; St Barnabas CE First & Middle School, Pershore; St Luke's C of E School, Maidenhead; The Boyle & Petyt Primary School, Skipton; The Forest Academy, Barnsley; Victoria Primary Academy, Leeds; Wallbrook Primary Academy, Bilston; Woodlands Infant School, Solihull.

All rights reserved. Apart from any use permitted under UK copyright law, no part of this publication may be reproduced or transmitted in any form or by any means, electronic or mechanical, including photocopying and recording, or held within any information storage and retrieval system, without permission in writing from the publisher or under licence from the Copyright Licensing Agency Limited. Further details of such licences (for reprographic reproduction) may be obtained from the Copyright Licensing Agency Limited, www.cla.co.uk

Typeset in India
Printed in the UK
A catalogue record for this title is available from the British Library.

Hachette UK's policy is to use papers that are natural, renewable and recyclable products and made from wood grown in well-managed forests and other controlled sources. The logging and manufacturing processes are expected to conform to the environmental regulations of the country of origin.

To order, please visit www.hoddereducation.com or contact Customer Service at education@hachette.co.uk / +44 (0)1235 827827.